Meandering

November, 2017

to Regina
you are an inspiration
through your writing
and your friendship

Meandering

Love
MaryEllen Lt.

Poems by MaryEllen Letarte

CW Books

Published by CW Books
P.O. Box 541106
Cincinnati, OH 45254-1106

ISBN: 9781625492531

Poetry Editor: Kevin Walzer
Business Editor: Lori Jareo

Visit us on the web at www.readcwbooks.com
Author's web site: www.maryellenletarte.com

Author photo by Latrice Cooper/Latrice
Photography

Cover photo by MaryEllen Letarte

For
Marie & Evelin & Gregory

In Memory of
Grandparents & Great Grandparents

Acknowledgments

Many thanks to the editors of the following publications where a number of these poems first appeared, some in a slightly different form and/or with a different title.

Mothersalwayswrite.com: "Great Grandma on Peggotty Beach"

Pitkin Review: "He Remembers SOS at High Ridge Conservation Area"

Sudden Marigolds: An Anthology of poems: "Ode to Blue," "I See You Again as the Hills Green," and "The Writer"

The Bay State Echo: "My Sister Found the Spot"

Thank You

To Jeanette Maes, president of the Massachusetts State Poetry Society and the Louise Bogan Chapter poets who encouraged me always. To Regina McGee and Christian Reifsteck who first read my manuscript and urged me to continue toward publication and to the leaders and writers of the many workshops through which I grew as a poet, particularly those at The Fine Arts Work Center in Provincetown and the Palm Beach Poetry Festival in Delray Beach. And thank you to the Goddard College Community, especially to Kenny Fries and Nicola Morris who believed in my work. And most importantly thank you to my dear family, whose love and support is immeasurable.

Table of Contents

Discovery

The cure is salt water
—a swish will do
or a sway floating on the Gulf of Mexico,
a rippled journey measured
by tears shed, rain endured.
I wind my way home
to myself.

I drink the wild air like a pilgrim
with no yesterday to return to
or tomorrow to work for.

I climb Mt Fuji, sail the Sargasso Sea,
find the lady slipper under the pine and
the truffle under the log.

I'm a dandelion on the wind
with my own sunshine,
my own navigation.

White Patch on Elm Street

I was the last one on the limb, the others climbed
higher in the old tree. They took a look at a patch
in the backfield, saw what they thought was
spring snow. The branch snapped and I fell, saw
blood run down my leg as I eyed the elm limb.
Dad carried me into the house (it must have been
Sunday) where he wrapped a towel around my
leg and we sped to the hospital. The doctor's skill
wouldn't pass Sewing 101. Stitches too wide, too
loose. No one will see this, he said. Miniskirts
weren't worn then. The scar is still there on my
thigh. It reminds me of the patch of white we
saw on the grass, not snow, but a calf born that
day.

yesterday's vision
tears cloud more than we know
elm trees felled by insects

The Icon

I

The portrait of the Madonna and Child was in my life from the beginning—the blue cloak, the sad eyes. It was ensconced in my family's living room, a sanctuary where we read, talked, took photos, welcomed Christians, Jews, and Muslims. We all sat there under the watchful eye of the "Blessed Mother, Our Lady." Mama cherished that portrait. When she grew old, it watched over her those last troubled days. In that lost portrait "Our Lady" was dressed like a peasant. She didn't have a halo. I don't know who claimed her.

II

The "Lady" is still grand in my mind, I'd like to know her title. It wasn't "Our Lady of Perpetual Help," though Mama called her that and I always needed help. She wasn't "Our Lady of Sorrows," although she looked plenty sorrowful. We schoolchildren were told that she cried for all the sins in the world, including ours. She wasn't "Our Lady of Victory." Who was she? She wasn't "Our Lady of Lourdes" or "Our Lady of Fatima." I wanted to meet those blue-cloaked ladies. "Queen of the Heavens" and "Our Lady of Guadeloupe," I first saw in a dusty museum. Could she be Maryam, Allah's mother? The Qur'an does mention her many times.

III

After I looked on the world-wide-web, I remembered I'd find her in my photo-album. She's there on the wall behind me in my wedding portrait. That's it! She must be "Our Lady of The Lake," the name of the church where I got married. Or maybe she's "Our Lady of Matrimony." After all, I've been married almost fifty years, someone must have guided me.

May

I hold my coat closed,
shiver in the longer days,
as the fuzzy, tree limbs
hail the red and green nodes.
Bushes expose their color
and robins pick up straw
to build their nests.

Trills, chirps, and peeps
return me to another May
when forsythia poked through
a cover of snow and cheered
my dying mother. She wanted
to stay to smell the lilacs,
to watch the fledglings.

"I'll miss you." She said.
And birds twittered as we
prayed, *Hail Mary full of grace.*

Ode to Blue

Without blue
would the jay be surprising?

Without blue
would the booby dance for his mate?

Without blue—
cornflowers and hydrangea
would shed their color,
Vermeer's Milkmaid and Picasso's
La Vie would dissolve,
the Virgin Mary would lose her cloak
and ancient manuscripts their tints,
the sapphire its light and stained glass
its glow.

Without blue
how would I see the rush of the seas
or the sky's depths
in your eyes?

Shoveling Snow Christmas Eve

Teenagers, we scooped layers of white
to free the station wagon
to attend Midnight Mass with our friends.
We found the church less than crowded,
unusual in those days—
an omen of empty pews to come.

I grieve for my youth, not for the Church.
Altar server and priesthood were closed
to girls. No chance to choose.
Maybe I would have accepted church vows
instead of traveling with children.

My holy orders became talks to myself
as I plowed into the winter of my life.
Today snow keeps me home, where I read
words of St. Francis Assisi and Agatha Christie,
then make snow angels with my grandchildren.

Meandering

I pulled weeds, when he could
no longer kneel. He pointed to the intruders:
chickweed, lambsquarters, and thistle.
As the sky grew violet we listened
to croaking frogs and katydids
before going inside to eat blueberry pie.

He didn't dance with me or Mom
at my daughter's wedding. He sat
in a gray suit and pink tie observing
his nine children.

At age twelve he was sent to the next farm
to keep the neighbor's barn,
to weed the garden and feed the sheep.
He ate his fill, drove a tractor
and sent money home to his mother.

When we walked in the conservation area he
talked of shooting squirrels and pigeons,
which his mother preserved in mason jars
to ward off winter hunger.

The Orange

When I peel an orange, each piece
releases the aroma of my mother and
her great granddaughter.

That day I gave one juicy section
to my mother, saved a slice for me,
presented the rest to my granddaughter,
who chewed and dripped, filled the room
with sunshine.

For one delicious moment we inhaled
the colors of the sun.

Red is the Color of Joy

My Grandfather Meets His Wife

The handy-man, Mr. Lewis, entered the paint chipped schoolhouse, stuffed leaky windows with cardboard scraps. He eyed the school marm, Miss Ruggles, as she directed her students. She's a natural, he said to himself. The youngest pupil squirmed, grasped a pencil, practiced printing while older students read Psalms from a black leather Bible. Others, close to graduating, sat in corners and wrote hero stories on unused newsprint-paper. Thank you, Mr. Lewis. Miss Ruggles said. You've arrived just in time to keep out the storm. The next day Mr. Lewis hummed, chopped wood and carried in logs, a chore the oldest boys relished, but not that day; Mr. Lewis did it. He wanted to say hello to the blue-eyed teacher. Miss Ruggles looked up as she glided toward her students. Mr. Lewis gave a nod, noticed her slim ankles. Good afternoon! She said, stunning as a cardinal in a winter apple tree.

Years Later

Handyman is not an easy career. Mr. Lewis and his family moved from place to place before settling on a farm in Wisconsin. Along with six children came failing health and desperation. By then my grandfather drove the tractor, planted seed, and pulled weeds, only in his memory. He sat on his gray-splintered porch, nodding to the mourning doves and to his gleeful daughter running toward mockingbirds. Grandma plowed straight rows from the high seat of the rusted tractor followed by her sons planting beets and potatoes. The boys learned to hunt as well as plant for winter eating. The jars of squirrel meat and pigeon looked gruesome lined up on cellar shelves beside the beets and potatoes. Exhausted from working morning to night, Grandma dreamed of teaching in the red schoolhouse. She prayed her daughter would have a better life.

Decades After

A red book with the worn embossed letters, The Poems of Oliver Wendell Holmes, arrived in the mail, a surprise from my brother wishing me a Happy Birthday. Inside the cover, a clear "Catherine Ruggles" is written. My grandmother read the Bible. I never heard her read a poem other than the Psalms; she must have cherished the Holmes volume or it would have gotten lost when she moved from home to home after leaving the failed farm. I wish I could thank her for saving the poetry book with the red cover. I'd ask her to read "Old Ironsides" and then share all those stories she began and never finished because her tears flooded them away, like the time she told me how she'd discovered her sister had died. She read it in the obituaries.

Great Grandma on Peggotty Beach

Great Grandma in her black-taffeta bathing suit
waded in the Atlantic Ocean,
before storms toppled the houses,
before sand washed into the marsh
and sent herons flying.

One summer I lived in a shore house,
struggled to swim. I wanted to wear long hair
knotted in braids, I wanted to float on the waves
like Great Grandma and her friends.

Buon giorno and buona sera were our
salutations.

Great Grandma and I gathered sand dollars
and other tide treasures, lost now like her stories.
I wish I knew why she had a cross blued on her
arm and why she burned it off.

I do know she arrived at the Port of Boston in
1913 with her thin sons. They learned English,
but she didn't. She expected to die young.

Women Wanted

In those days we prayed for children in China, donated our piggy-bank-savings. "Save the children! Send your pennies." The nuns echoed the missionaries. "There's not enough food, children have nothing to eat, nowhere to sleep. Some are left by the side of the road." Sacrificing didn't help but our pennies might have. Now the Chinese don't need money for food, they need brides for the boys not left by the side of the road.

cries confetti the air
two by two in the Ark
ten thousand mums

Marilyn Calls My Brother Godfather

He tells me:
"You can find anything
on the side of the road."

Today I found car mashed
potatoes, their eyes poking up.
Last week I found a pile
of clothes and shoes, not used
along with books and a prescription
bottle stuffed with marijuana.

When my brother taught English
to young people in China
he almost ignored
a most staggering find.
An eerie mew muffled
from a bush. He explored,
and found a baby with eyes
crusted shut. Neighbors pleaded.
"Leave her! Leave her!
She's sick," they said.
"She'll die," he said.

He and a friend carried the infant
to the police, then visited to be sure
she was cared for at the local orphanage.
His friend took her home
where Meimei became Marilyn—
adoption was easier then.

I See You Again as the Hills Green

You left us with the cold breeze,
             when green hills turned gray
             when deer slipped through
                  the horizon.
I won't give up,   you said.
    Wind   carried you away.
Yesterday the white-blossomed lilac bush
          opened a door
                to our youth
        where dogwood trees
        with their little crosses pinked
        where lilies of Easter forced into
        bloom sat fragrant on the sill.

Mom bought us pastel dresses
to celebrate the resurrection
of our back yard.

Fields and hills were our playground,
where you always took your doll and I
                my jumprope.
We licked our fingers after eating
blueberry jam sandwiches,
blueberries we'd picked together
on those warm summer days.

And in autumn when it rained,
we'd watch through our picture window:
        fruit trees ripen and thin
        and wind toss apples
           to raccoons who waddled away
           satisfied.

My Sister Found the Spot

They called her four eyes,
she struck out most innings
until one day she heard
the bat crack, saw the ball
soar and score after all
those fouls and strike outs.

One true hit was enough
to fall in love with the sweet spot
of that echoing crack,
but he cringed
every time he heard
that "confounded noise."

Tears gathered in his eyes
—I thought it was joy
at seeing his daughter finally hit the ball—
but for him the crack of bat against ball
sounded too much like a rifle.

Dad Remembers SOS at High Ridge Conservation Area

The sun is bright enough
to blind the ... --- ... tapping in my ears.

I saw seaman floating in Mae-wests—
yellow dots
          bobbed in dark surf.

Hundreds lost. ... --- ... lost.

          Our ship, SS Hartwell, steamed on,
                                        we
passed
          SS Brown,
                         our
                                  sinking sister ship.

I didn't do a thing but tap
... --- ...
          and tap ... --- ...   ... --- ...

I heard explosions and cries. Was it in my mind
or screeches in my headset?

Would we be next? ... --- ...   ... --- ...
          we steamed on, steamed on.... --- ...

He Talks to his Wife

"For you I learned to worry small beads
and to kneel by your side reciting
Hail Mary full of grace with our nine children.
I named my business Marian after Mother Mary.
But when our shop burned down
my faith incinerated. You understood
and cried by my side. You and your strong faith
embraced my war-torn arms."

"I'll drive you to St. Mary's and wait
in the car."

At My House

I
Doves coo me awake at dawn.
They glean the seed fallen
from the bird feeder
under blue-sky or gray.

II
Even the deepest snow doesn't
keep the Tom turkey away.
He uses icy mounds as step stools,
scoops the bird-feeder bare, then trots off.

IV
The radio blares, "Remove your bird-feeder!
Scattered seed attracts mice and chipmunks,
carriers of Lyme Disease."

V
I slather my skin with layers of insect repellant
and adopt a kitten who leaves pieces of rodent
at the back door and the chick-a-dee tweets.

Night Vision

I'd heard the crash and called 911 before I knew
the facts. Looking out I saw the thick oak fallen,
mangled on a red Mustang. The driver stepped
from the tangled mess. Not a scratch on his lit
phone (the police said later). He tapped as if he
were alone while owls shushed and sirens
screamed. Police arrived and wrote the facts on
thick pads but no remarks were asked of me (or
the owl). With a chain-saw a fireman buzzed the
old oak to full moon pieces while two workers
swept glass and twigs away. A flatbed driver
chained the mashed Mustang, then everyone
went home, except the owl. The next week I read
in the paper that the driver was cited for
excessive speed, Audubon crusaders wrote a
memo about saving trees, and the owl shushed
on my side of the street.

Late Celebration

No parades no stipends
greeted Dad in '46.

Though he Morse-coded through
U-boat explosions he was not
a veteran, the government said.

Veterans received assistance for college
and other skill building, not
the Merchant Marines.

Three children by 1946, his opportunity
came from looking ahead past science exams
and beyond broadside explosions.

In 1986 the government gave
the Merchant Men military status.
Dad was seventy.

Uncle Dick Talks About WWII

We enlisted after Pearl Harbor, not yet
knowing war horror. George, our oldest brother
stayed home to care for our mother and sister.

Your father lived through the most danger.

He joined the Merchant Marines,
trained at Gallops Island,
became a radio man on SS Hartwell.
If a U-boat had heard his dots and dashes,
you wouldn't be here.

I didn't want to go home maimed,
so I joined the submarines,
submerged in the SS Lionfish.
I was young and foolish.

After the war your father could have done
anything. His radio skills were sought but he
chose school, became a pioneer in the plastics
industry.

Your father lived through the most danger.

I miss him.

Isabel, Veteran and Poet

Isabel worked in India
caring for soldiers
and civilians with malaria.
She loved stories, tea with scones,
and writing poems.

When Isabel turned ninety-three
we dismantled her curio cabinet.
She gave me her memories
including a tiny wooden elephant,
a paper mache box,
and the most delicate item,
a limestone Taj Mahal.

Would India be India?

Would India be India without cloves and cumin
mixed with the ash of Varanasi?

without champak blossoms, their petals golden
as the sun?

without the sadhus and the towering temples,
oversized Buddhas, or street boys?

without the voice of Sarojini Naidu or the
songs of Tagore?

without ashrams and purple sari?

without yogis, quiet among the cacophony
of tuk-tuks and vans?

without the green on the banyon
twig or the red on the peepul tree?

without the shade of the Himalayas or
sacred cows roaming the streets beside
Muslim and Hindu?

Would India be India without tourists
like me who visit the Taj Mahal and sip
masala at every tea stall along the way?

On the Way to the Taj Mahal

A hint of masala and a sniff of mildew
greet me like musty books and spiced tea.

A skeletal horned cow sits on a trash heap
while two women in red saris
comb through yesterday's debris.
I capture a blur of red.

Wires dangle and twist across marble balconies.
Is this why the guest house lights flicker?

A sedan bashes a green, three-wheeled tuk-tuk,
its yellow roof flapping, as a human drawn cart
spills its coiled load of tan tubing. I gape
as traffic deadlocks, glad I'm walking.

Is it possible to ignore the street boys,
the chai stand, the legless
beggar, and flowing saris
on the way to the Taj Mahal?

Purple, white, and black turbans
divert my attention from the skinny dogs
that sleep willy-nilly on the street.

Rupees, rupees, a small boy bellows.
I take out a coin, place it in his dirty hand,
others, barefoot and shirtless, push toward me.

"Keep your pockets closed," the guide chides,
"look straight ahead, or we'll never
get where we're going."

Generations of Blueberries

I remember berry picking on the hill under the
high wires. On the hill where bugs buzzed,
     where briars bit, where berries
     stained me blue, but didn't stop my skin
     from pinking through.

I remember that first pie-taste of Mom's blueberry,
lush enough to stop the itchy bites and burning skin.

Is there anything sweet as wild berry pie?

My granddaughter's blueberry kiss.

Today at the farm plump berries
hang on wide bushes. Row after row
after row. They wait for my granddaughter
to pick and plop them in her plastic pail.

She is dazzled by neon signs that blink:
     ice cream, souvenirs,
     ice cream, souvenirs.

I buy her an ice cream cone and a ball
then wonder if she will remember the farm,
the blueberries, or me.

The Writer

He would have adored haiku,
jotting three lines on life's lessons
taking the last line from his weedy garden.

Villanelle would perhaps be a problem.
He'd compare it to a dog that grabs its tail,
not much discovery though lots of action.

Monologues would be his forte. They fit
his aptitude for writing letters as vehicles
for his hefty opinions.

Sestinas would have been his favorite,
long enough for a good story with gated edges
to keep the woodchucks out or in.

His free verse would be too terse
or maybe not—see the Gettysburg Address,
merely brief notes on brown paper.

And the sonnet! What's not to like?
He would have written sonnets to his wife,
his love for more than fifty years.

His sequence poems would be past and present
though future would be blank. His life was not
what he expected.

They Went Home

I miss the grandchildren, the blue sky, and sunshine. The spring has not opened its eyes. I want to see the peach fuzz on the trees and gold on the bushes. I want to feel the sun on my face and in my house. I want to rejoice in quietness, to hear titmice and sparrows chirp along with the nuthatch. They do not fly when I approach; they see that I'm the one who seeds the feeder. The roads are treacherous with winter heaves. I'm in the annex of my children's lives. I walk to wake up the poems locked in my cupboard.

purple sky silence
crows caw at mulching fields
the empty window

Thoughts After Viewing "My Studio," a portrait by Eleanor Norcross

A music score leans on a piano and
Eleanor's black robed father reads
a newspaper.

It would have been inviting if Dad
had played the piano or encouraged
music lessons. "Easy Listening" was his choice
when he sat clad in overworked boots
and a plaid shirt solving a puzzle in the newspaper.

He told me he dreamed of playing the piano.
Now when my grandchildren play
I see Dad in his recliner, listening.

A Smile for Sister Veronica

I

With oversized beads and cross swinging, Sister Veronica wrote on the blackboard. Spitballs and notes ricocheted in her crowded classroom. She grabbed her beads, turned, hummed, and intercepted a note, "I can write better with my toes than she can with her hands." I had boasted on that air-planed paper. Sister looked at me with eyes brown as my cocker spaniel's. "What's wrong?" She said. Not a hint of reprimand. She led me back to my seat and we all continued the Palmer Method of penmanship, arms in slow motion.

II

Sister took out her baton. "Every student will sing a solo this year," she said. I froze at my desk! On random days she would ask, "Who would like to sing today?" My hands remained by my side. When everyone (but me) was checked off in sister's little black book, she called my name. I stood up quivering, then sang a short song in a whisper. "Well done, would you like to sing another?" she asked.

Winter Wars

I'm lost in dark trees. No time for princess pine.
No sun for wintergreen to raise its plump arms.
Its roots war with pines, strong scents—mint and
pine. Birch bend heavy with frost while oak
leaves ice to black limbs. Twigs fall, velvet sound
when they hit the ground. Snow beards fir and
fur. Protons, electrons, rise, combine, collapse,
rejoin, unlink collection connection sparks not
war but new direction.

no one hears the link
wintergreen plumps
bonsai for summer

He Taught Me

Rounding the corner, I heard what sounded like crickets and tiny ting-a lings. Then I saw them, children riding tricycles with bells on their handlebars. They circled in an empty tennis court. A six-foot man encouraged the children, good job, stay straight, feel the wind, as they rode around the net. The children stopped and looked when the man left the court to get water from his van. The moment he returned they resumed pedaling. I never had a tricycle but I did get a bike on my tenth birthday, which I crashed racing down a hill that same day. No help from my dad then, he drove tractors not bicycles. My balance was bad and unfortunately has not changed since then, but let's skip that and go right to where my father was able to help me like that father helped his bicycling tots. It was in first grade. I believed books held secrets but I couldn't read. My father worked with me one letter at a time. The words looked too complicated to ever understand, but they snapped into focus and I read on and on.

awakening
dandelions, sunflowers
golden summer field

MaryEllen Letarte, a former dental hygienist, business owner, addiction counselor, museum fund raiser, author and poet, founded and directs the Louise Bogan Poetry Group, a chapter of the Massachusetts State Poetry Society. She grew up in Massachusetts amidst eight siblings, numerous aunts, uncles, cousins, and grandparents—all inspiration for her writing. After marrying she traveled widely, raised three children, and read nursery rhymes to her grandchildren. Through the years her articles and poems have been published in magazines and anthologies, and after earning an MFA in creative writing, she was moved to write poems that her great grandchildren would want to read for the sake of "discovering" their ancestors.